Stars can't shine without darkness

This book belongs to

____

Dont Be
Afraid to
Fail
Be Afraid
Not to Try

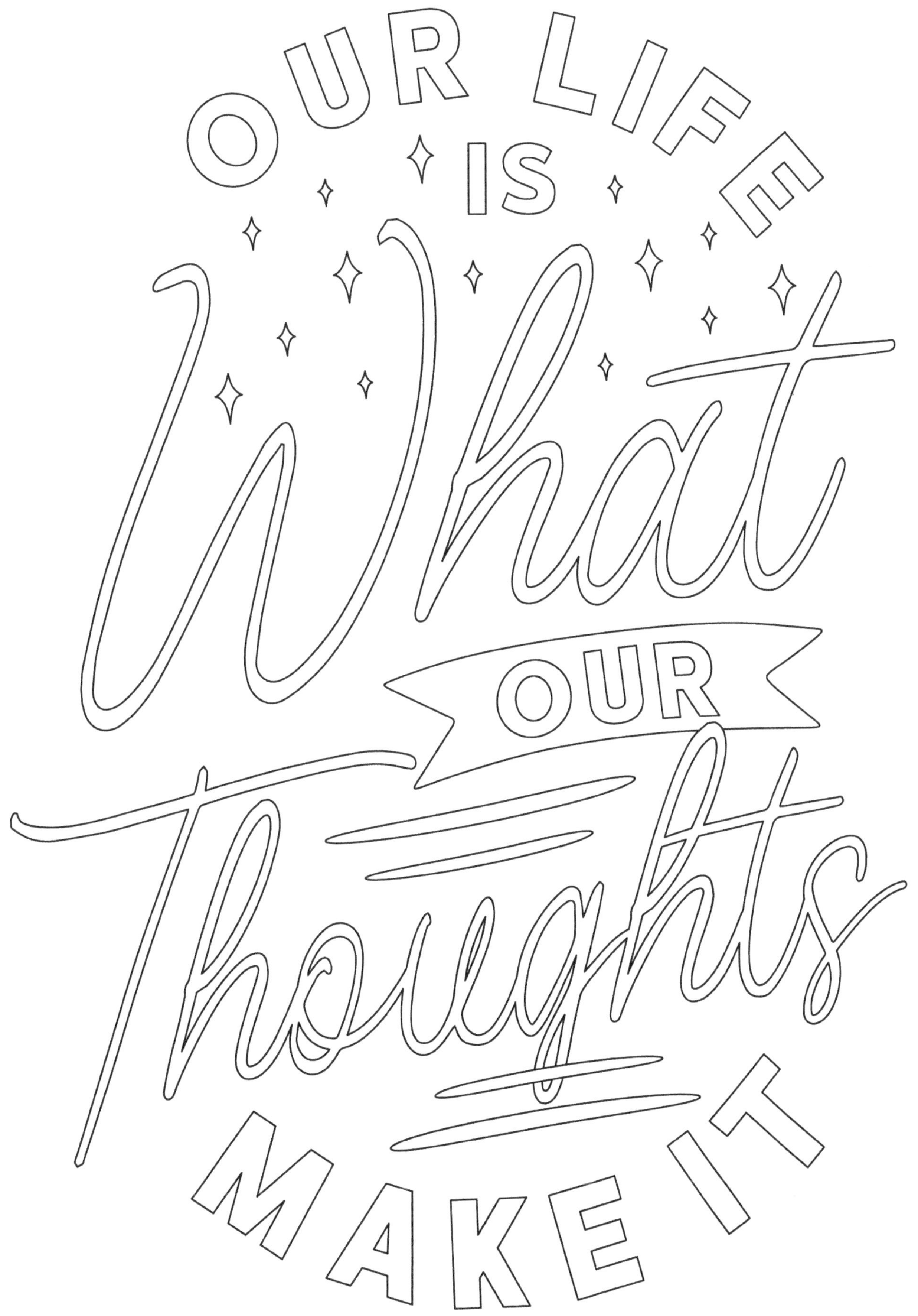

OUR LIFE
IS
What
OUR
Thoughts
MAKE IT

IT'S
Never
TOO
Late
TO START
Again

Stars
CAN'T
SHINE
WITHOUT
Darkness

It always
Seems
impossible
until
its
Done

Failure
Does Not
Define
Your
Future

The Harder You Work For Something The Greater You'll Feel When You Achieve It

IT'S
ALL ABOUT
- THE -
Process

Work Hard
Pray Harder

Let Life Surprise You

Life
is
short
make
it
sweet

WHEN LIFE GETS
tough
TAKE ONE DAY
AT A TIME

Do Good
and
Good Will
to
Come You

grateful

A Journey
of a
Thousand
BEGINS miles
with a
SINGLE
step

HAPPINESS IS NOT BY CHANCE but by CHOICE

Do Something AWESOME TODAY

STAY CLOSE TO
Anything
That
Makes
YOU GLAD

In
Difficult
Times
There
Is
Always
Hope

You
are
Somebody's
Reason
to
Smile

THE
SUN
WILL
RISE
& WE WILL
TRY AGAIN

Give Thanks With A Grateful Heart

THE BEST
VIEW
COMES AFTER THE
hardest
CLIMB

Don't Stop until you're Proud

Give
A HUGE
Impact
BY GIVING
A love
Words

You Are
Never Too
Old To Set
ANOTHER GOAL
OR TO DREAM
New Dream

You don't have to be perfect to be amazing

Always start your Day with A Cup of Positivitea

YOUR Best TEACHER is Your Last Mistake

No
PRESSURE
NO
Diamonds

DREAMS
DON'T
WORK
UNLESS
YOU DO

Don't Let Yesterday Take Up Too Much Today

This
Life
is
a
Gift

LITTLE
Things
MAKE BIG
Days!

be a
lamp
in a
dark
place

Stay
Positive
(Be)
Happy

You are Capable of Amazing Things

Lets START The JOURNEY Today

Do What is Right Not What is Easy

Share your lovely coloring
work with us:

Twitter @BeakyStarlight
Facebook @BeakyAndStarlight

© **Copyright (2021) by Beaky and Starlight Ltd - All rights reserved.**

This document is geared towards providing exact and reliable information in regards to the topic and issue covered. The publication is sold with the idea that the publisher is not required to render accounting, officially permitted, or otherwise, qualified services. If advice is necessary, legal or professional, a practiced individual in the profession should be ordered.

- From a Declaration of Principles which was accepted and approved equally by a Committee of the American Bar Association and a Committee of Publishers and Associations.

In no way is it legal to reproduce, duplicate, or transmit any part of this document in either electronic means or in printed format. Recording of this publication is strictly prohibited and any storage of this document is not allowed unless with written permission from the publisher. All rights reserved.

The information provided herein is stated to be truthful and consistent, in that any liability, in terms of inattention or otherwise, by any usage or abuse of any policies, processes, or directions contained within is the solitary and utter responsibility of the recipient reader. Under no circumstances will any legal responsibility or blame be held against the publisher for any reparation, damages, or monetary loss due to the information herein, either directly or indirectly.

Respective authors own all copyrights not held by the publisher.

The information herein is offered for informational purposes solely, and is universal as so. The presentation of the information is without contract or any type of guarantee assurance.

The trademarks that are used are without any consent, and the publication of the trademark is without permission or backing by the trademark owner. All trademarks and brands within this book are for clarifying purposes only and are the owned by the owners themselves, not affiliated with this document.

Produced by Beaky and Starlight Ltd.

Published : February 2021

ISBN:9798712627615

For more information about the publisher, please visit:

www.facebook.com/BeakyAndStarlight/

www.ingramcontent.com/pod-product-compliance
Lightning Source LLC
Chambersburg PA
CBHW080829260726
48654CB00027B/1802